LEARN TO LEAD

LEARN TO LEAD

© Copyright 2011

Jack B McVicar

freedomcentre Publishing

www.thefreedomcentre.com

ISBN: 978–0–9568–025–0-7

Printed in the United Kingdom

LEARN TO LEAD

JACK B MCVICAR

Dedication

To my wife, best friend, co-pastor and fellow leader, Sue -
your love, faith, friendship and loyalty is beyond
description. I thank God with all my heart for you.

To my children, Natalie, Charlene and Tanya, your
commitment and love along with your faithfulness to God
is such an encouragement. To Jon, Will and Pat, it's great to
have you in and around the family. To our grandchildren,
Ruby, Keyah, Caleb and Austin: we are immensely proud
of you.

To my mother and father who taught me how to follow
Jesus and to my sister Nancy and brothers Jim and Tom
who since an early age have encouraged their younger
brother by their example.

To everyone at the freedomcentre, thank you for being part
of the journey, the best is yet to be.

To my Source, Sustainer and Saviour, the Lord Jesus
Christ, what amazing grace!

To the hurting, distressed and broken hearted, freedom is
your destiny.

Acknowledgements

I am indebted to all who have played a part in the publishing of this book. First and foremost to Sue my wife for all her amazing input, ideas and suggestions, you have inspired me with your support and encouragement. Your creative fingerprints are all over this book.

Also the work of the media team at the freedomcentre, they have added value to the finished product. Matt Porter, Heather Barnes, Sam Lee, Josh Bedford and Paul Barber I appreciate all your hard work.

To those who have helped with the editing, Dave Cragg, Heather Barnes, Janet Barber, Ruth Carrington and Sam Lee, I am so thankful for all the suggestions and analysis. Thank you for your patience and persistence.

To Tanya my daughter for her photography.

To Peter Carrington who through his faithfulness, commitment and planning has helped make this and many other projects happen. I thank God for you.

I acknowledge all those over the years who knowingly or unknowingly have shaped me and my thinking, as all that I am and know is the sum total of all that I have been taught.

It is with deep gratitude I acknowledge our freedomcentre partners and in particular our vision team of Peter Carringtom, Tom Steward, Lydia Porter, Dave Cragg and Matthew Holman. Your constant sacrifices are being used by God to build the freedomcentre vision.

To Bishop T.D. Jakes, thank you for the profound influence on my life. You have helped enormously to unearth all that God has placed in me.

Finally to all who have endorsed this book, Rob Whittaker for his foreword and friendship, Nancy Goudie who I am proud to have as my sister, Clive Urquhart an old friend, and Philippa Hanna who attended the freedomcentre in the early days.

I have always been immensely proud of my brother and close friend, Jack, whether it was on the football pitch as a young boy when he was invited to take a trial for Celtic Boys' Club (his favourite Scottish football team) or whether it was through the enormous tough things he has had to deal with in life. He has much to give to others particularly in the area of leadership and I know you will discover gems of wisdom, real help and understanding throughout this very readable book.

NANCY GOUDIE – Director of ngm, author and speaker.

What a great book on leadership – simple, honest and profound. Learn to Lead takes you on a step-by-step journey to help navigate through some of the personal challenges of growing as a leader. With biblical principles and personal stories, Jack gives very practical wisdom and insight to inspire you to be the effective leader God has called you to be.

CLIVE URQUHART – Senior Paster – Kingdom Faith

I first met Jack in 2004 just prior to my dramatic conversion to faith. As a newcomer to Christianity I never expected to find such a parental warmth and nurturing from senior leaders. The passion that Jack and Sue have for their church family and their heart for the city of Preston helped draw me to faith. I'm always inspired by their passion to bring home the lost, and ever grateful for their influence in my life.

PHILIPPA HANNA – Singer and author

Contents

Foreword

by Rob Whittaker,
Principal Capernwray Bible College
Carnforth, U.K.

They say: 'The child is the father of the man', so in order to really appreciate my friend Jack McVicar, we have to go back quite a way!

I first met Jack when he was a leading salesman for Yellow Pages. Although the company modelled a step-by-step programme for signing up would-be customers, Jack related so well to people that clients often took out advertising packages during his first visit!

It wasn't long before the church, where I was pastor, deployed Jack as one of the key elders. I came to value immensely not only his loyal support, but also his uncanny instinct for knowing how to navigate tricky situations. Today, almost 30 years later, he is one of a small team of friends I go to for advice, when everybody can see the problem but nobody can figure out the answer.

I guess a significant window into someone's heart is to

look at the family they are part of. If you want to meet the 'real deal', I recommend you spend some time with Jack's wife and biggest fan, Sue. Or, failing that, you could track with one of their awesome daughters, each of whom is a living echo of their mum and dad's long obedience in the same direction.

A wise man once said that the person who never made a mistake, never made anything! Jack is refreshingly open about the times when his choices were perhaps, with hindsight, not the best. But those bleak times have been used by God to bring deep compassion and winsome tenderness into his portfolio.

Today, he and his wife head-up one of the new breed of churches which, in exciting and relevant ways, are carrying the kingdom of God to a new generation. Whether you encounter Jack and Sue ministering in the high school, which doubles as their church meeting venue, or on the other side of the world bringing blessing to desperately needy members of God's family, you, like me, will love them.

It gives me great pleasure to unreservedly recommend that you dig into this book. It flows out of Jack and Sue's walk with the Lord. It is full of wisdom and principles that I have seen fleshed-out in my two friends for more than a quarter of a century. If you enjoy it at least half as much as I have, you will embrace some key strategies for becoming the leader God intended you to be.

Rob Whittaker

February 2011

Preface

I had to learn to lead

Some leaders you meet will tell you that leadership is displayed from an early age; that it is shown from the playground at school and onwards. They will tell you leaders are born; that you have either got it or you have not. My experience is the exact opposite. At school I was not the leader! I was the best footballer, but not a natural leader. In business I was the best salesman in the company, but I was not the best leader. In fact my earliest experience of first-line management ended in my returning to sales after about six months, I hated it! I hated other people being in charge of my destiny; I quickly found out that, as a leader, your ambition and vision can be easily influenced by your followers. I objected to my team determining my rapidly reducing wage packet; I struggled with the fact that they had their own agendas and that I was no longer one of the pack. In short, I never saw myself as a leader at all.

All this changed when, at a very difficult and crucial time in our lives, God spoke to my wife and me and told us He wanted us to lead! I don't remember him asking, I just remember him telling us to begin the work of the vision that my wife Sue had held close to her heart for many years. This meant leadership; this meant total control; this meant learning to lead.

I don't know about you, but usually when God speaks to me about something or somewhere, He gives me a picture of the destination without seeming too interested in the details. It is almost as though He says: "This is where you are and here is where I am going to take you - work out the details!" Now, I know that God is intimately interested in the fine detail of our lives, but I also know that He wants me to grow and stretch, to realise all the potential that He has placed within me. He will not do the thing that I am able to do myself- He knows that we are far more capable than we think we are. If I am the only person who has experienced this then this book will be a small seller! However, I tend to think and believe that perhaps other people also need to learn how to lead themselves and others, as they head towards the destination that God has given them. They need to learn to lead in the detail of life.

I was interested to listen to former U.S. President George Bush recently, when he was interviewed by Rick Warren: He said:

> I was not a leader all my life; I had to learn to lead.

What you think of his leadership is not the issue here- there are many opinions on this. What I find interesting is that he had to learn to lead people.

This book is not about me, it is about you. It is about you learning to be what you never thought you could be: not a natural leader, but a supernatural leader; a leader who not only depends on natural skills, but depends on God's teaching and training, and who begins to believe and trust in God rather than man (or even circumstances).

As you begin to set out on this journey of learning to lead, I want to encourage you with one thought: in the Bible we see that God rarely picked natural leaders to lead

His people; He picked the people who thought they could never lead, never rule, never reign.

I think it is fair to say that, generally speaking there is an absence of good leadership within the church. There are many examples to the contrary but, across the board, we are weak in leadership. There are many managers who are administrating God's work, but not leading it.

Leaders change situations; managers keep things on an even keel. Leaders are brand new originals; managers are great at copying. Let's learn to be a leaders not copiers.

Introduction

A leader is not always the obvious choice

I love the story of David in the Bible and I have preached many times on the title "Are you a David?" David was up on the hills when the prophet Samuel came to town to anoint a new King to replace Saul. All of Jesse's sons from the oldest to the youngest, excluding David, were lined up to stand in front of the man of God. Jesse put forward what was humanly speaking the best for Samuel to pick from. The only one left out was David. David was only good enough for the sheep. David was left on his own, far away from the important business going on down at the farmhouse. What Jesse and his sons did not realise was that God had been preparing David privately for what He wanted him to do publicly. David himself did not realise the training he was receiving. He thought he was not good enough, was not educated enough, was not trained enough, or skilled enough. He probably thought nobody was interested in his abilities. However, he was wrong.

God was interested and He had already begun training David for what was ahead. While David was protecting his sheep, God had His own sheep in mind- the Israelite people. While David was killing lions and bears, God had a giant called Goliath in mind.

Look at Moses. Forty years in the desert, after killing someone. Moses was a murderer. Moses thought he was finished. There was a time when he saw himself as a leader but his humanity was too strong at that point. He needed time away from his people and time alone with God. After spending some considerable time at God's finishing school, Moses was ready for his graduation. He came across a burning bush which spiritually set him on fire for the task of taking his people on their own forty year journey with God. **A leader is always ahead of the people because of what he has experienced alone with God.**

David and Moses both had to do their learning when they

were out of the spotlight. They had to learn God's ways, His rules, and His supernatural leadership skills in the dark. **Never despise what God does with you in the dark - He is preparing you for the day when He will bring you into the light.**

With David it would lead to killing Goliath on behalf of a nation. With Moses it would lead to showing Pharaoh the tricks with his staff that God had shown him in the wilderness.

Do you understand what I am saying? He picked these people so that when they succeeded the glory went to Him and not them. I am always encouraged that Jesus picked such 'losers' and 'failures' as disciples, because if He could cause them to succeed, He can cause you and me to succeed too.

Most leadership books and self -help books I have read (and there are a fair few, as a glance at my library would tell you!) usually leave me with a sense of failure. Sometimes it is because I have failed to finish the book. Mostly it is because, having read someone's motivational thoughts and ideas, I have the depressing thought that I am not cut out for leadership. Have you ever had that experience - a sense of "it is OK for you; everything seems

to work out for you in your world"? If this is your
experience, then perhaps this book is for you.

I love what A W Tozer says about leadership:

> A true and safe leader is likely to be one who has
> no desire to lead, but is forced into a position of
> leadership by the inward pressure of the Holy
> Spirit and the press of the external situation. Such
> were Moses and David and the Old Testament
> prophets. I think there was hardly a great leader
> from Paul to the present day but that was drafted
> by the Holy Spirit for the task, and commissioned
> by the Lord of the church to fill a position he had
> little heart for. I believe it might be accepted as a
> fairly reliable rule of thumb that the man who is
> ambitious to lead is disqualified as a leader. The
> true leader will have no desire to lord it over God's
> heritage, but will be humble, gentle, self-
> sacrificing and altogether as ready to follow as to
> lead, when the Spirit makes it clear that a wiser and
> more gifted man than himself has appeared.

My experiences over the past 8 years of leading the
freedomcentre with Sue, my wife and co-pastor, have
taught me much about leading - both leading myself and

leading other people. I have learnt:

- Who and what to embrace and who and what to let go of.

- That not everybody who comes across your path is for you.

- That some people don't need to stay, for them it is best that they go.

- That other people do not want you to succeed; they do not want you to rise up and be what God is calling you to be; they have a different agenda.

- The gift of saying goodbye. In the early days of our church I wanted everyone to stay, everyone to be happy and no one to leave. That didn't last long.

- That not everyone who wants to travel with you wants to reach the same destination, and not everyone is willing to pay the price for the trip.

- To hold people lightly. It doesn't come naturally to me. I need His 'super' to go with my 'natural' in this and many other areas.

In this book I will share some of these areas with you. I will give you some important 'building bricks' that will enable you to become the leader you need to be. I want you to realise and recognise that you, like me, are capable of so much more than you could ever imagine.

I want in some small way to introduce you to the potential in you. I believe that if you could meet the other half of you, the part that God is working on right now, you would be amazed. There is another person within you that is just waiting; waiting for the moment to come when you are ready to let go- when you are ready to let God reveal, both to you and to a wider circle of influence, all that He has been working on.

It is my experience that somewhere deep down in everyone there is a masterpiece waiting to be revealed. It also has been my experience that life, circumstances and God will seek to chip away to reveal that masterpiece. Most people resist the work that is being performed in them, thus fighting the very thing that would ultimately display them in all their beauty and glory. **My desire, as we go through the seven principles of learning to lead, is to help your masterpiece be revealed.**

There are certain ingredients that can be added to and revealed in your life which will enable you to become all that you were created to be. I believe your destiny is ahead of you, not behind you. I believe that what is ahead of you will be better than what is behind you, but the preparation starts now. I believe God takes us from glory to glory (2 Corinthians 3: 18). He is always looking to progress our lives, to take us to the next level. He is a forward thinking God.

I believe this book will show you how all you have gone through in the past and all that you are going through now can be used to reveal and progress your future.

When Michelangelo was asked about his masterpiece 'David' he explained that the sculpture had always existed within the stone. He had simply chiselled away the rock around it. You might think you could never lead, but somewhere deep down there is a desire to influence and direct people. The problem is you feel you are not able. This book is for you. It is a book for those of us who feel that deep down there is a something greater to be released.

God is the master sculptor, you are the stone. Are you prepared to be revealed? I believe your best days are ahead of you. Are you ready for the journey?

David had no idea. Moses had no clue that his best days were ahead of him. God was not finished with them, He had only begun. You will have better days ahead than you have experienced up to now, but you must learn to lead!

I love the following poem:

Whom God Chooses

When God wants to drill a man,

And thrill a man, and skill a man,

When God wants to mould a man

To play the noblest part;

When He yearns with all His heart

To create so great and bold a man,

That all the world shall be amazed,

Watch His methods; Watch His ways.

How He ruthlessly perfects

Whom He royally elects!

How He hammers him and hurts him

And with mighty blows converts him

Into trial shapes of clay

Which only God understands;

While his tortured heart is crying

And he lifts beseeching hands!

How He bends but never breaks

When His good He undertakes,

How He uses whom He chooses

And with every purpose fuses him;

But every act induces him

To try His splendour out....

God knows what He's about.

Anon.

I have endeavoured to make this book an encouraging book. It has never been my objective to amaze you with my intellect (that would be impossible!). What I want to do is convince you that you have something to offer in leadership in the area where you work or serve. If you find that hard to believe, so much the better.

In this book we will look at **seven principles** to learning to lead:

1. Learning to have a great attitude

2. Learning about your vision

3. Learning to love people

4. Learning to fail properly

5. Learning to be relentless

6. Learning to trust

7. Learning to grow

Chapter One

Learning to have a great attitude

Attitude is usually seen as a critical word. We talk about the attitude of a teenager, a sales assistant, a waiter or a waitress. They have an attitude. What we mean by that is that they were (or perhaps still are) 'difficult'.

It seems they have a huge chip on their shoulder, something against the whole world, and they are going to take it out on you. They have the same abilities as everyone else, as many gifts as other people, but their attitude stinks. They are going nowhere because the emotional baggage they are carrying is too heavy.

As Christians we are told in Philippians 2 that our attitude should be exactly the same as Jesus! We should have a 'supernatural' attitude. The verses at the beginning of the chapter tell us just what this was:

> v3-4: Let nothing be done through **selfish ambition** or conceit, but in lowliness of mind let each **esteem others** better than himself.

That tells me He was extremely **SELFLESS**

> v6-7: who, being in the form of God, did not consider it robbery to be equal with God, but **made Himself of no reputation**, taking the form of a bondservant, and coming in the likeness of men.

That tells me He was absolutely **SECURE**

> v8: And being found in appearance as a man, **He humbled Himself** and became obedient to the point of death, even the death on a cross.

He was willing to be **SUBMISSIVE**

> v9: Therefore God also has highly exalted Him and given Him **the name which is above every name**, that at the name of Jesus every knee should bow.

He was and is eternally **SIGNIFICANT**

However for most people the 'natural' temptation is to be

and therefore become:

- •SELFISH

- •INSECURE

- •DOMINEERING

- •INSIGNIFICANT

I believe there is a part in all of us that wants to have the supernatural attitude. Often life with all its burdens, pain, responsibilities and challenges drives us towards the natural attitude. It takes the supernatural Holy Spirit living in our lives to enable us to change.

The truth is: we all have an attitude. What that attitude is will determine how we get on with other people and how much we will achieve with the gifts God has given us. Natural gifts don't guarantee success. It is only when your gift is married to a great attitude that you start on the journey to success. If you find that you are constantly having fights and difficulties with people and that everyone you meet or have dealings with seems to want to argue with you, guess where the problem is? It's with you!

One thing is for certain: you cannot lead people, especially in a voluntary context, with a bad attitude.

Matthew 7:12 says our attitude determines how we relate to people. It tells us to treat others in the way that we ourselves would like to be treated:

> Therefore whatever you want men to do to you, do also to them, for this is the Law and the Prophets.

The reason the verse says this is because that is exactly what happens. People will give you a smile when you smile; people will frown when you frown; sometimes people will even laugh and cry when you laugh and cry. They mirror you. You yourself dictate other people's reactions. If you don't believe me, try one day to have a smile on your face constantly and see what happens. You might want to try complimenting people as you meet them and see what happens. People react mostly, they do not act.

The attitude you have currently has been determined already. That is the bad news! The attitude you have currently can be changed and developed. That is the good news!

David the Psalmist says in: Psalm 139 :13-14:

> For you created my inmost being; you knit me

together in my mother's womb. I praise you
because I am fearfully and wonderfully made; your
works are wonderful, I know that full well.

We all start from different places. When I was a boy at
school, the teachers - in order to make a race really
competitive - would give us a staggered start. This meant
that the fastest runners had a start line much further back
than the slower runners. The slower runners, depending on
their speed, would progressively start from positions nearer
and nearer to the finish line. I am not particularly interested
in where someone is in the race of life, what interests me is
how far they have come!

Perhaps you are behind me, because you started much
further from the finish line. You may nevertheless be
running much quicker than me and might very soon be
passing me.

I don't know what sort of start you had in life. In one
sense it doesn't matter, because your attitude will determine
how you finish.

While teaching leadership in India recently, Sue and I,
along with the team who travelled with us, met an elderly
couple in their eighties. This couple, who pastor a church,

rise around 4am every day and walk two hours to attend a prayer meeting. After finishing their time praying, they go on to visit and pray with some of their congregation, before making the two-hour walk back home. This is their every day experience. Their attitude was so positive, so genuine and so real that their faces shone and radiated God's grace.

I remember thinking: If Christians in the West could have just half of this positive attitude and commitment we would not be living in such a negative environment.

When travelling in Africa we often see a much more positive attitude to life than we see in the U.K. They have so little, but when we preach and teach we see a hunger for learning and for leadership skills that is often sadly absent in Europe. They are not just hungry physically, but they are hungry to learn as well. Their attitude is far better than their circumstances might lead us to expect.

The Bible says ALL of us are fearfully and wonderfully made. God took a look at you when you were born and said "WONDERFUL!"

It doesn't matter what your parents or siblings said - God was very pleased. David in the Psalms says: "I know that full well!" Do you?

What is your attitude towards you? Do you like yourself? Do you enjoy spending time with yourself? If you don't, then why would other people you seek to lead like you and want to spend time with you?

Another lesson we need to learn is how to get on with other people. Other people are here to stay. There will always be other people in your life. How you act, react and your attitude towards them will determine your success in leading them.

Teddy Roosevelt said:

> The most important single ingredient to the formula of success is knowing how to get along with other people.

So if attitude is vitally important, what then can I do about my attitude? Well, you can improve it in several ways...

You can improve it by deciding who to spend time with.

People say that where and with whom you live affects your attitude. That is quite true. So, who do you live with and where do you live?

Do you live and spend most of your time with negative

people? If you do, most likely they are making you negative.

Do you live and spend most of your time with 'can' people or 'cannot' people. The 'can' people's first inclination is to tell you 'you can do it', whilst the 'cannot' people say 'you cannot do it'.

Whoever you are choosing to spend your time with, remember that they are having an influence over you. Be careful who you choose to invest your time with.

It is one thing to be kind to people; it is another thing to **choose** a negative person's company. You cannot always choose your relatives, but you can choose your friends. Choose wisely.

My mother used to tell me to stand on top of a table and try to pull someone else up to where I was. She wanted me to see how difficult it was to pull other people up to where I was, compared with how easy it was for them to pull me down. The only person who finds it easy to bring us up to His level is Jesus and even He had to come down to our level to make that happen.

It is only when there are enough people pulling a person up that it becomes relatively easy. We always say to people joining the freedomcentre: if they will plant themselves in the soil that God has placed us in, their attitude will change and their experience will alter. We are able to pull up the person who needs the breakthrough because there are enough of us who have experienced a breakthrough into freedom for ourselves.

We have seen over and over again people's attitudes change; going from negative to positive the longer they stay with us. Is it because we are miracle workers? No! It is because we have introduced them to the positive Kingdom of Jesus Christ. The Kingdom that Christians are a part of is a positive one, not a negative one.

As a Christian the only way you will catch the attitude of Jesus is to spend time with Him. If we catch negativity by spending time in the wrong company, then we will catch a positive attitude and we will become selfless, secure and submissive, as people and as leaders, when we spend time with Jesus.

You can improve it by letting go of your past.

Let go of your hurts, pains, disagreements, mistakes and anything that you see as negative in your past. Philippians 3:13-14 tells us to be 'forgetting those things which are behind and reaching forward to those things which are ahead, I press toward the goal for the prize of the upward call of God in Christ Jesus!'

I don't know what you have gone through. I don't know the hurts you feel. I wasn't there when you were abandoned, rejected, forgotten or abused. I don't know any of your experiences, but I do know you need to leave them behind. You are not doing yourself any favours by carrying them on your shoulders. That load is too heavy for you. That load was never meant to be carried, it was meant to be abandoned in your past.

The truth is: you need to forgive and forget. You need to travel light if you are going to learn to lead. There are many people out there, some you know, some you don't, who are waiting for you to 'lighten up' and help them. We cannot carry someone else's bags for a while, to help them, if we are weighed down with our own bags. Drop the bags rather than drop your shoulders. Let go of your past.

You can improve it by speaking to yourself.

One of the ways of leaving our past behind is talking to ourselves. Do you talk to yourself? I do and you should too. Just make sure that you don't answer yourself back - it's not a good sign!

Truth is we talk to ourselves all the time, we are just not very good at it. We speak the wrong language. We speak negatively and we constantly put ourselves down. We need to learn how to speak positively and creatively to ourselves, to add value instead of devaluing ourselves. What you think of yourself is revealed by how you speak about yourself.

Proverbs 23: 7 says

>   For as a man thinks within himself, so he is.

We need to stop our 'stinking-thinking!' It creates a future which is negative, filled with fear and not worthy of who we are and what we can become.

We need to start **'strategic thinking!'** That is thinking that the best is yet to be; that our latter days will be greater than our former days (Job 8:7); that God has plans for us- plans to prosper us and give us a hope and a future. (Jeremiah 29:11)

Shut up about what you are not, and

Speak up about what you are.

Say after me:

> God has plans for me.
>
> Plans to - bless me.
>
> Plans to - give me a hope.
>
> Plans to - give me a future.

He has not finished with me. The days ahead will be better than the days behind as I trust in Him.

We all can have times when we say we are not what we want to be, but we need to learn to speak up about what God says we are.

Have you thought recently about who He says you are?

Look at what He says:

- you are the head and not the tail-you are above and not beneath (Deuteronomy 28: 13-14)

- you are a son or daughter of the King of Kings and Lord of Lords (2 Corinthians 6:18)

- you can do all things through Christ who strengthens you (Philippians 4:13)

- you are more than a conqueror (Romans 8:37)

- you are a joint heir with Christ (Romans 8:17)

- you are free from condemnation (Romans 8:1)

- you are the apple of the Father's eye (Psalm 17:8)

- you are being changed into His image (2 Corinthians 3:18)

That is who you are, and a whole lot more, according to the Bible. Concentrate on your positives and stop thinking about your negatives. You are not what he said, they said, she said: you are all that God says you are, nothing more and nothing less.

You have abilities and gifts other people long for. You are special. You have been made in God's image. You are not a mistake or a disaster; you are strategic - strategically placed for such a time as this. Take your attitude, give it a brush up, give it a remodel and start to become the person you were created to be. No matter what age you have reached, it's never too late. You are alive; that means God has a plan for your life.

You can improve it by adopting God's plan for you

Yes, God Himself has a plan for your life. You may feel you are going nowhere and that nothing is working out.

You may feel that you take one step forward and two steps back. I have news for you, God does not go backwards. Nothing is ever a surprise to Him. He is never on the defensive. He even knew you would buy this book and read it. If God has a plan for your life, wisdom would say: "Buy into that plan!"

Over the years of leading the freedomcentre, people have sometimes accused me of stopping God's plans for their lives or not allowing them to be all that God wants them to be. The problem is, if I can stop God's plans for someone that makes me God. I may be able to stop you, but one thing is for sure: I cannot stop God! If God wants to promote or demote anyone, I cannot stop Him. Whoever God wants to bless, He will bless and no man can stop Him. He will find a way where there is no way. He will get the blessing to you and through you. If that is true (and it is) it would be wise for each one of us to adopt His plan for our lives. Follow that plan. Have faith in that plan. Commit to that plan and stop thinking that any man or woman can control your destiny.

In the U.K., where a road is private, belonging to some individuals or landowners, that road must be maintained by the owners. They are responsible for the maintenance and upkeep of the road. They are financially responsible, they are personally responsible. When that road is adopted by the council, the council then becomes financially responsible, the upkeep is their responsibility. The maintenance is then up to that authority.

While your plans are your plans, you are responsible for them. They are your financial commitment. You have to upkeep them. It is all down to you. However, God has adopted us as His children, we are His, and all He asks is that we accept His plan. He will pay for everything. Nothing is too expensive. If something needs to be done, provision is there. The responsibility is His.

As we understand and accept this truth our attitude changes. It matures, it relaxes, it accepts and it submits.

We cannot Learn to Lead if we are not willing to be led! God wants to lead us. Good leaders are great followers! Good leaders have a great attitude. You can learn both. You can learn to go from having a bad attitude to a good one and then from a good attitude to a great one!

It doesn't take brains, it doesn't take brawn. It takes bravery! You can do it - God knows you can!

QUOTES AND NOTES

Seven quotes on attitude

1. The only disability in life is a bad **attitude**.

Scott Hamilton

2. Ability is what you are capable of doing; motivation determines what you do; **Attitude** determines how well you do it.

Lou Holtx

3. **Attitude** is a little thing that makes a big difference.

Winston Churchill

4. The winners edge is not in a gifted birth, a high IQ, or in talent. The winners edge is all in the attitude, not aptitude. **Attitude** is the criterion of success.

Denis Waitley

5. Excellence is not a skill, it is an **attitude**.

Ralph Marston

6. Whatever things are true, whatever things are noble, whatever things are just, whatever things are pure, whatever things are lovely, whatever things are of good

report, if there is any virtue and if there is anything praiseworthy—meditate on these things.

Philippians 4: 8

7. The longer I live, the more I realise the impact of **attitude** on life. **Attitude**, to me, is more important than facts. It is more important than the past, the education, the money, than circumstances, than failure, than successes, than what other people think, say or do. It is more important than appearance, giftedness or skill. It will make or break a company, a church or a home. The remarkable thing is we have a choice every day for the **attitude** we will embrace for that day. We cannot change our past, we cannot change the fact that people will act in a certain way, we cannot change the inevitable. The only thing we can do is play the one string we have, and that is our **attitude.** I am convinced that life is 10% what happens to us and 90% of how I react to it, and so it is with you...we are in charge of our **attitudes.**

Charles Swindoll

Seven notes on *attitude*

List seven points from the chapter on **attitude** which have struck you most and which you want to remember:

1..
....
2..
....
3..
....
4..
....
5..
....
6..
....
7..
....

.

Chapter Two

Learning about your Vision

Where there is no vision the people perish.

Proverbs 29: 18a (KJV)

Maybe you are asking, 'What is vision?'. What I mean by vision is an anticipated or imagined goal or project. What would you try and do if you knew you would not fail? What is in your heart to do for yourself, your family or God? What do you feel God has revealed to you?

Eric Liddell, the Scottish Olympic runner said: "God made me fast and when I run I feel His pleasure."

God made you, and there is something that happens

when you do what is in your heart to do; you also feel His pleasure and experience pleasure yourself. People recognise that gift in you and, some may even encourage you. That gift will take you to your vision. As you develop and train your gifting, ideas and thoughts of what could be will begin to enter into your mind. You will imagine yourself in certain situations and at certain events. That is your vision.

Is your vision bigger than you? Great leaders set goals they **cannot** finish. What I mean is this: that they do not merely consider their own lifetime, but also think in terms of generations. Their desire is for their vision to continue growing long after they have passed from this life. Why just impact your own generation? We should aim to impact the next generation and the one after that.

People take a look at your vision, then take a hard look at you and decide whether they want to be on the journey with you. If they do not buy into the vision or buy into you, they will not join you on the path you are treading. People want to follow someone who knows where they are going. Are people following your leadership? If not, they have decided either against you or the vision. Maybe it is because you do not yet know or are not totally convinced yourself where you are going. You need fixing!

Do you know where you are heading? A leader should always have a vision. If one vision falls through or is obtained, it should never be long before a leader has another vision, another plan and another dream. If you have a dream or a plan or a vision it demonstrates that you have something to work towards and lead others to.

If the vision tarries or is delayed, wait for it. Do not run ahead thinking you are going ahead; reality dictates that you are going nowhere.

Wait until you know where you are destined to go.

Before you start storming off into the future physically, go there in your mind, go there spiritually. Place yourself in front of God, before you place yourself in front of man. Ask God questions about the vision, so you have answers when man asks.

God often delays telling us our destination so that He can first work on us, before we set out on the journey. It is always better to repair a car before a journey, rather than let it break down after a couple of miles and then get it fixed.

Sue had a vision for many years. Occasionally she would try and begin to start out with it but it was never quite the right time. It looked right physically, but it wasn't right spiritually. She carried this vision for about 20 years before God spoke to both of us, saying it was the right time, spiritually, to begin. God knows that it was not the right time physically to begin, but God does not look at the physical; He looks much deeper than that. When we began many people told us it was the wrong time, but we knew it was the right time. Our vision is the freedomcentre. The vision was Sue's, but the timing belonged to God. He knew when we would be ready, as a couple, to birth it.

Leadership involves pain as well as privilege, moreover part of learning to lead is showing you can suffer pain before you ever come to enjoy privilege. In our private lives we both proved to ourselves and to God that we could endure pain. That is good preparation for leadership.

As we saw earlier, David the Psalmist was up on the hills, Moses was out in the desert; you need a place too. It might be in a job you hate; it might be in unemployment; it might be with people who don't understand you. Wherever it is, let God fix you before you start fixing anything or anyone else. There are already too many leaders out there who only last five minutes after setting off, because they did not prepare themselves. They did not get in front of God before getting in front of man. It took Moses forty years before he was fixed and ready for action.

I remember so clearly, when I was in business, having many 'fixing' moments with God.

One time I moved from a very successful job selling Yellow Pages advertising space. With the promise of more money ringing in my ears I moved to a company which sold office equipment. At the interview everything sounded just great, but it was only a matter of days until it dawned on me that this was a bad career move.

What I didn't realise at the time was, a bad career move sometimes means a good God move. Why? Well, because of this move I suddenly went from being in charge of my life, with all the benefits of being very successful, to not being in charge, having no money and feeling very vulnerable. I still remember driving to my place of work with tears in my eyes, pleading with God to "get me out of this"! Have you ever done that? Tried to do a deal with God? If He will get you out of this or that situation, then you will make some sacrifice that you think impresses Him.

God doesn't take you into trouble in order to sort you out. We are perfectly capable of doing this for ourselves. What He does is wait for us to run out of solutions and ideas.

Then, lovingly, He steps into the trouble to repair us and sort us out.

It is a bit like having a car that we never service or repair. It is only a matter of time before we end up at the garage. When we arrive, the mechanic identifies what we feel the problem is, but he also brings to our attention other problems, which are the result of our neglecting to perform maintenance.

A wise mechanic will use the opportunity to fix our other car problems whilst he has it under his care.

So it is with God. He looks for opportunities to 'fix' us because He loves us so much. We come to him with this and He deals with that. With God, the issue is usually not the issue. He sees much deeper than our superficial problems. God is big on preparation. He will take as long as required to prepare you for your destiny.

Jesus was 30 years in preparation, and for Moses it was 40 years.

Bible students take 3 years for 30 years ministry; for Jesus it was 30 years preparation for 3 years ministry. The point is neither how long you prepare; nor the duration of your ministry. What counts is what you accomplish.

Preparation is the secret to success.

People say to me "I have a vision, what should I do with it?" My answer is:

Write it down, **read** it and **act** on it!

- **Write** the vision down. The Bible tells us in Habakkuk 2: 2 "Write the vision and make it plain on tablets, that he may run who reads it."

- **Read** it and reread it. Let it read you. Know every part of it. Know it back to front. Consider it, pray about it and study it. Ask others to read it; ask their opinion and advice. Decide whether you are ready to pay the price that the vision demands. If someone asks you about it, you should know it back to front. You should be able to give an account of it.

- **Act** on it. As soon as you are convinced by God about your vision, begin to put one foot in front of the other. You may be hesitant, you may be scared, but do it. Start to pay the price for it. Act! Don't wait for God to move your foot; you move it. God guides moving people rather than immovable objects. We all know if we break down in our car, it is much easier to push it when it is moving rather when it is still. Momentum is key, start working on the plan. Heaven alone knows where this will take you, but what you can be sure of is that your attitude will change as you adopt His plans for your life.

Other people say to me, "I don't have a vision; where can I find one?" My answer and my experience tell me: the vision may be closer than you realise. Perhaps the vision has found you.

Your situation, your friends, your experience, your gifts and your abilities do not exist by accident, they are there by design. Even your mistakes, hurts and pains are allowed by God, for Him to use for your future. He tells us that He works all things together for good.

So, get alone with God and let Him show you His vision for your life:

- **Why** were you born?

- **What** are you gifted at? There are some wonderful books that help you decide what you are naturally gifted at. There are also books which will help you determine your spiritual gifts. I would recommend you buy these and see what they reveal.

- **Who** has He brought into your life to lead and to follow?

- **When** does He want you to begin?

- **Where** should you be?

- **Should** you stay or go?

Spend time with Him and the vision will become clearer. He may use His word to speak to you; He may use other people to guide you; He may give you a burning desire to buy into someone else's vision, to support them and enable their vision.

The vision I am working for every day was first given to Sue. You do not have to have a vision which is only for you. Your vision can be to take on board someone else's vision. You can enable, develop and bring into being a vision which was first received and developed by another leader.

In fact I would go as far as to suggest that you need to follow someone else's vision, before you lead your own. Serve their vision like it was yours. This will teach you so much. You will learn what it feels like to be a follower. Serving another's vision will teach you loyalty, commitment, honour and love. It will teach you servanthood and integrity. If you can be true to someone else's vision, you will remain true to your own. Do not see these years as wasted, but as seeds sown, which God will bring to fruition. Sue and I served three different ministries before having our own. We did everything that could be done to support the leaders of these ministries, to enable their vision to occur.

The experience we gained in this was invaluable. The price we saw those leaders pay meant that, to a certain extent, we knew what was ahead. Of course, leading rather than being led is always a different experience. However, the experience we gained was nevertheless a great help.

If you can be a great follower, you can be a great leader.

If you are an average follower, you will be an average leader.

What I am saying is: mostly, you will need to learn to

follow, before you learn to lead.

A word of caution: as you follow someone else's vision, be careful that you do not cause division. It is very easy to cause division, without even realising it.

My experiences indicate that most people do not set out to cause division; nevertheless division still happens and it is never easy for all concerned.

What causes it? Here are some of the reasons and things to be on your guard against:

- misunderstanding

- disloyalty

- lack of communication

- lack of love

- mistrust

- different destination

- selfishness

- envy

- greed

- lack of information

- lack of understanding

You can only walk together with people when you share a common destination. As soon as the destination is different there comes a fork in the road where there is a parting. That parting should be recognised and positively dealt with. There is nothing wrong with saying goodbye. Some goodbyes are positive for all concerned. It means both parties can go towards their own destination. If you are one of the parties involved, always take the high road.

Take the road less travelled. What I mean by that is, don't put yourself first. Put the vision, God, and the Kingdom first. Jesus said "Therefore whatever you want men to do to you, do also to them, for this is the law and the prophets." (Matthew 7:12)

Over and over again in the New Testament Jesus did for others what they should have been doing for Him. Watch how He washed the disciples' feet.

Another example from the Old Testament is how Abraham dealt with Lot. When the time came for separation between them, Abraham offered Lot the choice of which piece of land he wanted. In doing so, Abraham trusted God to look after him. When you read Abraham's story you see that this is exactly what happened – God richly blessed Abraham for his obedience and Godly attitude.

As you lead your vision, whether it is a personal vision or a corporate vision, you will find that from time to time people will come along seeking to divert you slightly from your course.

Your decision is to decide whether they are proposing a:

- good move

- great move

- God move

If it is either a good move or a great move, forget it. If it is a God move, go for it. That is easy to say and difficult to perceive.

Experience tells me that the best way to decide is not to rush into the decision.

First of all ask God.

Secondly ask your leadership team, co-leaders, close

friends etc.

Thirdly pray and ponder.

What I have experienced is that God **always** has your best at heart and **sometimes** man does too.

Before you make the change ask yourself some questions:

1. **Who** is suggesting it? Take a long look at the person who is proposing the change and take a view on them. What is their track record? What relationships have they had in the past? What happened in those relationships? How wise have they been with them?

2. **Where** will the new course take me? A few degrees change now may mean a huge change down the line. Is that where God told me to go initially? Has God changed His mind?

3. **What** will be the ramifications for me and for others if I change course now? Who will be hurt and how will I deal with that hurt?

4. **Will** other people follow this new direction?

Let me finish by saying this: usually there will be **no** change. Sometimes the advice of a change of course is a diversionary tactic. The proposed new course, if followed, would often cause a division. It is like when you are travelling on a journey and this is the first time on a particular road. You may stop for directions; after receiving them you continue travelling following the new advice. After travelling a little way down the new track, somehow you just know that you are on the wrong road. That's when the conversation in the car can get a little heated, because everyone has an opinion. Sometimes the refusal to change course with the vision will cause division anyway, so do not be scared of that decision. A vision cannot have two destinations.

In some cases there may not be two destinations; rather, two or more routes that can take you to the single destination of your vision.

In other words be careful to understand the difference between advice that would:

- Change the journey.

And advice that would:

- Change the destination.

There are many ways to reach the same destination. The route can be up for discussion; the destination, most times, should not be. You can go the scenic route, the fast route, the easy way or the hard way. Just make sure you get there. Don't argue about detail. You only have so many arguments in you, so keep your powder dry for what counts.

Thomas Jefferson said:

> In matters of principle stand like a rock, in matters of taste swim with the tide!

In other words, don't get into every decision in fine detail, just make sure you are going in the right direction. If the consensus of your people is to have a few days of a scenic route, don't argue, go with it. It's more important to have them happily on board and going in the right direction, than lose them because you always want to be on the fastest route.

All the way through this journey, with all the discussions and people coming and going, you will be deciding just how desperate and committed you are to your vision. How keen you are to get there. How much you want it. Is it worth it? Only you can answer that, because ultimately you are the one that will pay the price, because it's your vision.

QUOTES AND NOTES

Seven quotes on vision

1. To grasp and hold a **vision**, that is the very essence of successful leadership—not only on the movie set where I learned it, but everywhere.

Ronald Reagan

2. **Vision** is the art of seeing the invisible.

Jonathon Swift

3. Leadership is the capacity to translate **vision** into reality.

Warren Bennis

4. People buy into the **vision** before they buy into the leader.

John Maxwell

5. Give to us clear **vision** that we may know where to stand and what to stand for – because unless we stand for something, we will fall for anything.

Peter Marshall

6. Indignation and compassion form a powerful combination. They are indispensable to **vision**, and therefore to leadership.

John Stott

7. Where there is no **vision** the people perish.

Proverbs 29:18

Seven notes on *attitude*

List seven points from the chapter on **attitude** which have struck you most and which you want to remember:

1...
....
2...
....
3...
....
4...
....
5...
....
6...
....
7...
....

.

Chapter Three

Learning to love people

People are made in the image of God. The more you love God the more you will love people. The problem is some people want to make it very difficult for you to love them, or so it seems. They will make life as difficult as they can sometimes, usually not intentionally. Love them anyway.

The mistake we often make as we learn to lead is that we try and:

- like them instead of

- loving them

As a leader you are not called to like everyone you lead - that would be impossible. However, we are called to love them.

Loving people means:

- sacrificing for them

- serving them

- seeking the best for them

- saving them from themselves and their past

It does not mean always:

- keeping them happy

- telling them everything

- being their friend

- responding to their every need

Learning to lead is about learning to love. If you want to love someone more, there are a number of things you must do:

1. Spend time with them

2. Seek to understand them

3. Sacrifice yourself for them

4. Simply pray for them

If you do these four things, very likely your love for them will slowly begin to grow.

It is very hard to spend time with someone, seek to understand them, be willing to sacrifice yourself and pray for them every day, and not begin to love them.

If you love people you will find it so much easier to lead them.

When we are leading, we are in the 'people business.'

People can be:

- tools

- trainees

- terrorists

- teachers

Tools

If people believe in you, they will invest in you, they will resource you and they will submit to you. They will be like a tool in your hand for you to use. The saying is 'a bad workman blames his tools'. A good workman may not always have the best tools but he will adapt and use a tool that isn't quite right and make something of value. A really good workman will look after his tools and will even be able to repair and restore them. Those who have learnt to lead will protect and look after their tools-their people. They will, if they are wise, learn to value them, use them and create with them.

They will not use a hammer to saw wood. They will not use a chisel to tighten a screw. They will not use a paint brush to sweep the floor. All of these examples sound ridiculous, but so is using people in areas where they are not skilled. Some tools are multi-purpose and can be used for different tasks - some people are just like that. You can put them to work in two or three different situations. Generally, however, both people and tools have a specific use.

In the early days of a ministry or vision, people often have to be utilised in multiple ways because the needs demand "all hands on deck". However, that should only be for a season: if you are still in this mode ten years into a vision, then something is wrong. From my observations of Jesus and my own experience, a leader has to step in to do the jobs others will not, or cannot do. Two examples of this from Jesus leadership are:

1. **John 13:** No one else washed the disciples' feet. Jesus the leader, the servant leader stood in the gap and performed the task, he then told his disciples to serve each other with the same servant heart that He had demonstrated.

2. **Matthew 14: 21:** Jesus healed the man's son. The disciples had not yet got the faith to perform the task that needed performing, so Jesus stepped in.

   As you learn to lead and as your people learn to follow, there will be times when you are doing jobs that don't make sense, that others will struggle to understand, that you yourself will find frustrating. All the time you serve however, you are learning to lead and you are teaching others what true leadership is. If you are the type of leader who will not deign to dirty your hands or serve those who you are leading, you will produce leaders who will not sacrifice for those who are following.

Everyone is a tool in your hand. Use them as skilfully as you can and to the extent that their character and ability allows.

Trainees

People are your trainees and apprentices. They will generally be willing to submit to you, as long as they feel they can learn something from you. Your job is to always be spiritually one step ahead. Very rarely will someone follow you if they know more than you. If such a person does follow you then you have a very special person on your team! Those people who do not know as much as you, and who are willing to learn, are your trainees.

These trainees are your investment in the next generation. They are your children and, God-willing, will produce your grandchildren. They need to catch your DNA, need to learn your passion, your conviction and what is important to you. However, be aware that they will learn your faults too, so be honest about them. Then they can ignore your faults and concentrate on everything positive.

Trainees are generally younger than you. This gives me an opportunity to talk about age! Generally speaking the people who will follow you and submit to you will be younger than you. In our experience at the freedomcentre, it's the young whom God has brought along to be trainees in our ministry. I thank God for them. They are younger in their faith and younger in years. They, like the disciples, have plenty of faults and rough edges, but what they lack in experience they make up for in readiness to serve.

In your vision, look for people who will:

- listen to you

- learn from you

- love you

Our experience is that, in the main, these qualities have been demonstrated by the younger people. We also have a number of our own generation and a few older than us whom God has brought along to balance out the average. We have so needed them. You will too. They have different gifts and abilities. They might have money, where younger people have time. They might have experience, where younger people have enthusiasm. They might have endurance, where younger people have passion.

Terrorists

We live in a world where terrorists are the greatest threat. When you take on the vision God has given you, I believe Satan unleashes terrorists who will, at a moment's notice, unleash the enemy's power against you.

Sometimes that terrorist is **within**

Sometimes that terrorist is **without**

Within

The most dangerous terrorist is someone who lives within your community and shows no sign of being your enemy. They are sleepers, awaiting the call from their master to begin wrecking that which they have lived with.

Not everybody that is with you on the journey is for you!

If you don't believe me, have a look at Judas. He was called by Jesus, lived with Jesus, slept with Jesus, ate with Jesus, did miracles with Jesus, but ultimately was not for Jesus. When the call came, he was willing and able to betray Him.

Terrorists are dangerous people. Love them anyway. Serve them anyway. Trust them anyway. Why? Because one day they will drive you towards your destiny. The astounding fact is Jesus washed Judas's feet, but Judas was a terrorist used by the enemy of our souls. The amazing thing is he was used by our God to drive Jesus towards His destiny. He drove Jesus towards the cross.

As you learn to lead you will discover that your terrorists will always drive you towards your destiny. Don't be frightened of them, it's a set up; God has a plan. He has a plan to bless you, give you a hope and give you a future; and your terrorist will be part of that plan. Don't fear because the terrorist is near; rather, be thankful Jesus has a plan. That plan is for you to Learn to Lead and achieve all that God has put within you heart.

There is another terrorist: the terrorist within the leader themselves. We normally call this our weakness. We call this our situations. We call this our past, our heritage, our nature. This terrorist will seek to kill you, given half the chance. The good news is you know this terrorist; you don't need anyone to tell you what they are. The bad news is sometimes we try and justify and accommodate this enemy. Never make it your friend. Never get comfortable with it. Never trust it. Never make allowances for it. It will kill you if you let it. Therefore you need someone who loves you

and is committed to you with whom you can share your
wounds. We may be leading, but sometimes we are
bleeding and need someone experienced in leadership and
the things of God, who will, with careful expertise, stop the
bleeding and nurse us back to full health. One thing you do
not do is bleed all over the sheep. You are there for them
not the other way around. Many a leader has died in the
arms of the sheep when they should have been nursed by
the shepherd.

Without

You will always have snipers who will try, with their
opinions and their arguments, to put you off your stride.
They will try to take you down and out by their terrorist
activity. These are people who will not pay the price you
are paying and who will not join you on your journey.
Sometimes they are jealous of you; sometimes they are
competitive; sometimes envious. As with the enemy within,
love them anyway. I love what Jesus said on the cross:

"Forgive them Father for they know not what they do!"

That is the truth. Most people who give you a hard time
on the journey have no idea they are being negative,

obstructive, and difficult, or that they are sucking the desire and life out of you.

They don't know you; they hardly know themselves. They are fearful of their own future and they don't want anyone else to reach out for theirs. When they criticise you and offer their 'advice' they have no idea what they are doing. Usually they have never led anything or had responsibility and so don't understand the weight you are carrying. If they had, they would help to serve you by helping to carry the load rather than putting more weight on you. Some people feel they know better and want to share that better way with you. That brings me onto the next group...

Teachers

You don't know everything about everything! You don't need to!

Your people can be the greatest teachers in your life. Sometimes you need to drop the pretence that you know everything and learn as you lead from those who are following you.

God has brought them into your life as **tools** and as **trainees** and even sometimes in exceptional cases as

terrorists but He also can use them as **teachers**, to teach you.

Everyone you have in your organisation knows something that you don't. They are an expert in something. They are not with you by mistake. They have been planted there as a teacher in some area, for you to learn from. Learn from them as you lead.

If you will let them, they will teach you. They will empower you; they will promote you; they will follow you and protect you. The Bible encourages us to be "submitting to one another." (Eph 5: 21)

You can learn to lead as your people resource you in your journey.

This is part of loving people: releasing what is within them and letting them know that they are valuable and appreciated by you.

So tell them and show them by your words and deeds.

- If you are a **Pastor**, sit, listen and take notes when the people with teaching ability in your church are speaking. It is good for you to listen and learn; it is good for the teacher to see you take them seriously; it is good for the church to see you are teachable. It is also good for you to have a Sunday off and still be in church. It may be a workplace for you but it is also the place where you worship. Also, Pastors - while I am speaking directly to you - make sure you are 'giving' to the church and 'loving' your wife. Some Pastors get confused and they fall in 'love' with their church and 'give' to their wives. God hasn't called you to love his bride, that's His job; your job is to serve the church and go home and love your wife.

- If you are a **married man**, listen to your wife! Really listen to your wife. She has been strategically placed by God to teach you, as well as to learn from you. She can teach you all about your blind spots. She can educate you about the people who are following you, good and bad. She can show you situations from a feminine perspective. As I have been writing this book, Sue has at, various times, shown me areas where I have missed the mark.

- If you are a **married woman**, listen to your husband! When he shares something listen to him. A masculine outlook is something he can add to you. If he is a good husband he will want to protect and care for you. If he is a spiritual man he is head of your home, I believe. You may lead the vision but God has placed him as head of the home. Let your guard down with him and let him be all that God has purposed him to be in your life

- If you are **single**, make yourself accountable to someone of the same sex. A more mature person than you are, spiritually and probably physically. Spill the beans with them. Be honest and vulnerable. Share your aspirations and disappointments. Bless them, give to them and encourage them for all they do in their leadership. Don't just be a taker, be a giver too.

- If you are a **business leader,** make sure the main thing is the main thing. Don't be like a greyhound chasing a metal rabbit round a circuit over and over again, while other people benefit from your energy. The greyhound is sweating and exhausted while the bookmaker and the gamblers make and lose money on the greyhounds back. Make sure you are benefiting from your business. Yes of course you should encourage and remunerate your employees properly, but also make sure your family and your loved ones see some benefit from your endeavour.

I remember my mother and father going on holiday and meeting a man and his family. He was a businessman who had driven himself hard at business for about ten years without ever taking a holiday. This man had sacrificed everything to build a business to the detriment of his family and his health. About three days into the holiday my mother came down for breakfast to see an ambulance taking away the body of a man who was obviously dead. After enquiring, she was told it was (you've guessed it) the man who had sacrificed it all for his business. If you having a business means only that your family never see you and that you die early from a heart attack, then you have failed, no matter how much you leave in money, stocks and shares. Don't climb the mountain of success only to see your family at the bottom looking at you from a distance, both physically, emotionally and spiritually.

Every one of your employees can teach you something as well. They have resources, capabilities and contacts that you don't immediately see. You may have hired them for one reason but you will find, if you look carefully, that they can teach you about other things. They will have hidden resources that they don't realise or understand the value of. It's your responsibility as a leader to find them.

The main objective as you gather people around you, to work and complete the vision you have, is to find people who will join you on the journey and who will:

Complete you, not Compete with you; there is a world of a difference.

When someone wants to serve you with their advice, thoughts, and guidance, they will do it away from the 'heat of the battle' and from behind the trenches. Beware of people who will not pay the cost of the fight, but who will tender their opinion anyway. They might not realise it but they are not serving you; rather they are trying to sink you.

No one likes an armchair critic- people who pontificate, and tell you how to do it and how not to do it. The only problem is they will not lift a finger to help you. The truth is these people are trying to 'lord' it over you and they have trouble serving you. Anyone who wants to serve you will offer their advice and continue working. The sign that they respect your leadership is that they keep on working, whatever you decide to do.

The way to get the best out of people in the project or vision you are trying to accomplish is to love them. Sometimes you will feel the love you give is rebuffed; more often you will receive a harvest from it. The majority of people respond positively to genuine love. Loving people will earn you the right to lead them.

QUOTES AND NOTES

Seven quotes on loving people

1. We reach our best, and we do our best, we are at our best in a **love** atmosphere.

E.W. Kenyon

2. Management is doing things right; leadership is doing the right things.

Peter Drucker

3. **Loving** people live in a **loving** world. Hostile people live in a hostile world. Same world.

Wayne Dyer

4. To live without **loving** is not really to live.

Moliere

5. The best portion of a man's life: his little, nameless, unremembered acts of kindness and **love**.

William Wordsworth

6. The greatest possession we have costs nothing, it's known as **love**.

Brian Jett

7. If we **love** one another, God abides in us, and His **love** has been perfected in us.

1 John 4: 12

Seven notes on *loving people*

List seven points from the chapter on **loving people** which have struck you most and which you want to remember:

1...
....
2...
....
3...
....
4...
....
5...
....
6...
....
7...
....

.

Chapter Four

Learning to fail properly

I want to be positive about being negative. When you read your Bible you discover that many people we associate with success also failed.

Noah was a drunk

Jacob was a liar

Gideon was afraid

Rahab was a prostitute

Jonah ran from God

Samson ran after women

Peter failed by denying Jesus his Lord

These are just some of many, but they became successes because of God's grace and because they learned to fail properly.

You are also going to fail sometimes, get over it! Learn from it and move on. Everyone fails, but not everyone recovers from their failures. If you let it, failure will be a stepping stone to your success.

Success will teach you some things; however, if you let it, failure will teach you everything.

Every one of the disciples failed, but only one failed to learn from their failure. All the rest learned, moved forward and achieved great things for God.

I have failed so many times. Let me share a simple illustration of just one of these occasions.

In the early days of the freedomcentre we were miraculously given use of a four storey office block building in Preston. The rent was about £85,000 per year. As you can imagine, for a church just in its infancy this was impossible. Nevertheless, God made the impossible possible and we got the building rent free.

We were there for about three years, during which we performed our first baptism. We decided to use a birthing pool, which we could fill up and have the baptism inside. I read the instructions (honest I did) and it said it would take two hours for the pool to fill. Because I like to multi-task, I decided that I could visit the local supermarket for ten minutes in the meantime, to buy some sandwiches and a newspaper.

While visiting the supermarket I met some old friends and we got talking and time passed. I knew I had been longer than ten minutes - it was probably more like thirty minutes (honest!). It was when I opened the sliding door into the main reception, upon my return, that I knew something was wrong. You see, the water was flowing towards me. As I came in, it was going out.

As I walked over the spongy carpet and through into the downstairs room (thankfully) that the baptism pool was in, I realised that I had failed...big time!

Operation clean up started and carpets needed to be ripped up and floors mopped out. What began as a simple task of filling up a pool became an expensive carpet refurbishment and tidying up process. I can still picture the church squelching over wet carpet the next day wondering what on earth they were walking on.

How do you see failure? Depending on how you **see** failure will determine your success.

●Failing at something doesn't make you a failure

●Failing in the past doesn't mean you will fail in the future

●Failure is not avoidable

●Failing prepares you for responsibility.

If you are going to achieve anything in your career, in your home, in your family, in your church and in life in general, you will have to learn to fail properly.

There are 3 rules when dealing with failure:

1. Acknowledge it

2. Act on it

3. Avoid that failure in the future.

1. Acknowledge it

All of us, when we were young, remember saying, "it

wasn't me!" when we were confronted with a wrongdoing.

We knew it was us; and other people knew it too. We knew the evidence all pointed in our direction and yet we stuck to the story "it wasn't me!".

We simply would not acknowledge what everyone else knew: it was me. For many of us this response of denial became a habit and, having become adults, when confronted with failure either by circumstances or by an employer, we simply revert back to our childhood pattern and say "it wasn't me!"; only perhaps in a more sophisticated way. As adults, what we tend to say is, "it wasn't my fault because..." Then we find a reason that suggests the fault wasn't ours. The problem is nobody is fooled.

I remember so well when I was 16 years of age and desperate to drive. Everyone was out of the house and the car in the drive was crying out "drive me". It didn't need to cry out to me for very long before I had heard and responded. Next thing I knew, I was driving up and down the small drive at my parents' house- that was, until I crashed into the garage! After noticing some slight damage to my parents' garage, I quickly put the car back to where it was originally parked and returned to what I should have been doing. Comfortingly, my parents never noticed, or so I thought, and life went on. The problem was, they did notice and someone else noticed too.

Some years later I was listening to Selwyn Hughes speak about moving on from failure, and he asked us to pray and ask God to show us a couple of things that we needed to repent of. Guess what God brought back to my memory? Yes, you guessed it: the drive, the car and the damaged garage. Next time my parents visited, I spoke to them about it and asked their forgiveness. I cannot tell you the blessing God brought into my life because of that simple act. It set me free in a way that I had not experienced before.

Choosing to acknowledge a failure does not make you a failure. In fact, in God's eyes it makes you a success. He deals in failures, He is used to it and He has made provision for it. However, He cannot do anything with people who will not acknowledge their failure.

Every situation is different and God deals with everyone in a personal way. I prayed that God would show me two situations where I needed to ask for forgiveness. In reality He could have shown me many, many more situations. These two were like a token of the others.

Would you list two things where you feel like you have failed?

1...

2...

For some of you reading this book, this is the first time you have acknowledged these failures. That is the first step forward from failure to success. In acknowledging it to yourself you have taken a major step forward.

Now can I suggest you take a further step in the right direction?

Acknowledge it to someone else, but not just anyone.

Find someone you trust, someone who has proved themselves trustworthy in your life, perhaps a friend, a Pastor, a Minister, your husband or your wife? When you have chosen that person, carefully sit down with them, somewhere in private, and share these "failures".

The Bible says: confess your sins to one another. Acknowledge to them your failure. If you do this and if the other person is honest with you, you will learn a few things:

- You are free from that failure

- You will see it in a different light

- You will discover everyone fails

- You will deepen that relationship.

2. Act on it

Now, what are you going to do about it? By failing, you discovered one way not to do it! You discovered one way of not accomplishing your goal. You discovered a route never to waste your time going down again.

There is so much action to take after failure, but the most important action is to get up and try again immediately.

There is a Chinese proverb which says:

Failure is not falling down, but not getting up.

One of the most common comments a driver makes after having a car crash is: "I don't want to drive." The sensible ones get behind the wheel and leave the crash behind them. Perhaps the crash was their fault, their failure, but it doesn't make them a failure! Failure is to pick yourself up, dust yourself down, and start all over again.

It doesn't matter how many times you fail your driving test, what matters is when you pass. Your driving licence will never say how many times you sat the test; it will simply say that you passed it. Should you ever be unfortunate enough to be stopped by the police, you may be asked for your licence. However you will never be asked how many times you failed your test. If you failed to re-sit the test then that would mean that you remain a failure, but sitting it and re-sitting it until you have passed, makes you a success.

Most people deal with failure in a way that is negative. Their attitude is 'I tried it once' and they then let that one experience determine their future. Maybe once is not enough, maybe you need to try again, and perhaps again and again, until you learn all the ways you can fail at something until you succeed.

Action does so many things:

- It leaves the past behind, it leaves the last failure behind, and

- It projects you into your future

- It takes you nearer to success.

3. Avoid that failure in the future

Your failure has taught you something. It has taught you a way <u>not</u> to get the job done. It means you can avoid that way in the future. This is called learning. Learning to fail properly! So avoid that pitfall and move on. There will be a temptation in the future to fall down in that area again. If you have:

- Acknowledged it

- Acted on it, then that will encourage you to

- **Avoid it** next time.

Whatever area you fail in can become an area of strength in your life. What I mean is this: if you handle the failure positively and properly you can avoid it in the future.

If I drive into a pothole in the road, it bursts my tyre, it causes me to lose time, it means I have the expense of a new tyre and the pain of changing it by the side of the road.

The next time I drive along that road, guess what I will be looking for? I will look out for that pothole and, when I see it, I will remember the pain and the financial loss, and the hole will definitely be avoided.

That is the attitude to have to the failure you experienced. Failure is to know the pain of the last experience but avoid it in the future. You can fail positively by putting into practice what you have learned from the past. Failure can make you stronger, wiser and a better leader.

Zig Ziglar (American motivational speaker) said:

> Failure is a detour not a dead-end street.

C.S.Lewis (British scholar and novelist) said:

> Failures are finger posts on the road to achievement.

Failure tells me you are trying. The man or woman who never tries never fails; and fear of failure stops many people from trying. Failure tells you that you are going somewhere. You have a target, a destination which you are trying to reach. Failure tells you where your destination is not; it tells you where the target is not to be found.

Thank God for failure, it is a stepping stone to where you want to be. It is not a red light: rather it is an amber light telling you to get ready to go.

As I end this important chapter on failure I want to tell you a story about me which will hopefully encourage you.

Thirteen years ago at the time of writing, my business partner and I were dealers in property. At one stage we sold a number of properties to a businessman from London. (One day, Sue and I may write the story of the freedomcentre and tell the whole story of what happened during that time.) A number of months after the sale had completed, my partner and I were sued for £1.25 million. The repercussions of this were enormous to our family and also to my partner's family. The businessman who we sold the properties to went to the High Court in London and got a freezing order on our business affairs. Our bank accounts were frozen; we were not allowed to deal in property or, for some time, to draw money out of our accounts. This all happened one Thursday afternoon, the day before Good Friday when Sue and I were due to lead the Easter services at our local church. The effects of this action on us in our business were enormous: our banks withdrew support from us, loans were drawn in, we could no longer afford our outgoings such as mortgage payments etc.

With everything else that was happening at that time this was the biggest challenge of our lives.

The years since 1998 until the present time have been a long walk back from the brink. Personally, and as a family, we found out who our friends were. We also discovered much more about each other. As a family we went through it together. It brought us closer. We were five years into this struggle when God told us to start the freedomcentre. Naturally speaking, it was the most inappropriate time to start a church and a vision: however it was the most supernaturally appropriate time.

To the outside world it was failure, but to God it was potential. To God we were clay in the Potter's hands. He had finally got me in the place where I had no room for manoeuvre. I had to let Him take control. It was physically and emotionally the hardest time in our lives, but it also was the most rewarding time spiritually.

I know what failure looks like. I know what it is like to want to be set free from circumstances beyond my control.

I know what it feels like when people judge you wrongly and make judgement calls on what they feel God is doing in your life.

I also know that God knows even more about you than man does; and He still loves, cares for and protects His own.

With God, failure is never ever final! With God failure is a starting line, not a finishing line.

I only tell you this because I want you to understand and take this on board: you have a chance to succeed no matter where you have been. No matter how dire the circumstances, no matter how bad it looks, God has a way through and a way out. I know that. My family knows it, and I want you to know it too.

Trust me my friend; I know He can do it for you too.

QUOTES AND NOTES

Seven quotes on failing properly

1. There are no secrets to success. It is the result of preparation, hard work and learning from **failure**.

Colin Powell

2. I've **failed** over and over and over again in my life and that is why I succeed.

Michael Jordan

3. A life spent making mistakes is not only more honourable but more useful than a life spent doing nothing.

George Bernard Shaw

4. You always pass **failure** on the way to success.

Mickey Rooney

5. **Failure** is simply a price we pay to achieve success.

6. Success is the ability to go from one **failure** to another with no loss of enthusiasm.

Sir Winston Churchill

7. The steps of a good man are ordered by the Lord, and He delights in his way. Though he fall, he shall not be utterly cast down; For the Lord upholds him with his hand.

Psalm 37: 23-24

Seven notes on *failing properly*

List seven points from the chapter on **failing properly** which have struck you most and which you want to remember:

1..
....
2..
....
3..
....
4..
....
5..
....
6..
....
7..
....

Chapter Five

Learning to be relentless

If there is one chapter I have a special affection for, it is this one. If the past has taught me anything, it has taught me, sometimes through painful moments, this major lesson.

> Gifting will never be enough to get you to your future.
>
> Ability will get you some of the way.
>
> But it will take relentlessness to get you there!

Wherever you are headed, if it is a dream worthy of the name, you will go through difficulties, upsets, problems and situations. If you are not prepared to be relentless you simply will not make it.

Bishop T.D. Jakes was once asked by a young man heading to go into ministry for one word that would sum up what he would need to be to succeed in his new vocation. After thinking for some time, the answer he gave, to sum up all that this young man would have to be was:

RELENTLESS!

That one word will shape and determine your destiny. It will determine whether or not you achieve. It will determine whether you pass or fail, whether what is in you will come out, or stay inside of you, whether your marriage fails or succeeds. Whether your company takes off, or stays on the ground. It will mean that you will Learn to Lead your life or your vision rather than giving up and settling for the mundane.

That one word, if applied to you and your situation, will change your life.

●**Relentless** in your passion for God.

●**Relentless** in your desire to succeed.

●**Relentless** after making mistakes.

●**Relentless** in the midst of the storm.

●**Relentless** when all others are giving up and giving in.

●**Relentless** when you don't feel like it.

And what is true of the young man is true of me and is true of you. If we are going to get to where we want to be, we are going to have to be relentless.

If your desire and dream is to have a successful marriage you will need to be relentless in your love for your partner.

If your desire is to have a successful business, you will need to be relentless in your drive to make it happen.

If your desire is to lead a successful organisation, you will find that plans and preparation are not enough. Some days you just have to be relentless. Nothing else will do.

The road to success is tough; it is lined with potential hazards and problems. Life has a way of testing you to see how much you want it and see how much you will sacrifice to get it. If you are not relentless it will find you out that is for sure.

The decision has to be made now, right at the start of the journey. The decision has to be made every day, all the way through the journey.

In 1993, after many months of training, I ran the London Marathon. During this training period I learned that in order for me to run the 26.2 miles I would have to be relentless. Whether or not I felt good; whether or not I felt like running; whether the weather was good or bad; whether people ran with me or did not; whether or not I had the time. I had to be relentless or the mission and the goal of running in that special event just would not happen.

During that period in my life, there were times that I just did not feel like running. On one occasion near to the date of the race I was ready to do my trial run of approximately 20 miles. Sue was ready and willing to come out to deliver some refreshments to me at about the 13 mile mark. We had devised a plan that she would drive alongside me as I ran along. At about the right time I finally saw her coming up behind me and she had the passenger window down ready so she could pass the much needed drink to a parched and half dead runner. The problem was as she drew up alongside me, every time she leaned across the passenger seat to hand me the drink her other hand was turning the steering wheel and was turning the car into me and nearly driving over me. I didn't know whether to laugh or to cry! One thing that was for sure though, I was not stopping. I never did get that drink.

'Why did you continue?', I hear you say! The reason I went through with it was I had said I would do it. People knew I was training for the marathon and I had made a commitment to do it.

When the going gets tough and all you want to do is settle, the decision has to be made that you will see it through.

The temptation will always be to:

- **Settle** for just enough, when God wants you to have more than enough.

- **Settle** for so far, when you haven't gone far enough.

- **Settle** for good, when great is round the corner.

- **Settle** for 'learning' when God wants you to

become a 'teacher'.

- **Settle** for second best when best is just in reach.

If the good news is that you have a vision, the bad news is you will have to be relentless to make that vision happen.

If the good news is that you are gifted and talented, the bad news is that you will have to be relentless for that gift or talent to be enjoyed.

If the good news is that God has given you direction, the bad news is it will take you being relentless on the journey to reach the destination.

Success doesn't equal gifting, it usually equals being relentless. There are some very exceptionally gifted people who have got nowhere. They never developed relentlessness in their lives.

Gift and ability are not enough! Where I have succeeded in life, I have been relentless. Where I have failed, I have relented. I have given in against the pressures, the criticism, the hurt, the pain and – yes - the failure.

Giving in is short changing yourself!

Giving in is robbing yourself of your future!

Giving in is to deprive yourself of the success which may be just round the corner!

Can I encourage you; whatever it is that you dream of, wherever it is that you want to be, do not let fear of failure, the constant sniping, criticism or lack of finance and resources wear you down. Go to God - who is in Heaven and who will work all things together for your good - go to Him and ask for the strength for the journey and decide once and for all that you will make it, you will get there, you will succeed and you will be relentless.

This attitude is needed most of all in the Christian church and in our Christian walk. Many Christians have a conditional attitude to their faith: "If God will answer my prayer, if God will show me the way, if God will makes things happen for me - if He gets me out of this mess - *then* I will believe, then I will serve, then I will give, then I will trust."

I believe God looks for people - God looks for leaders - who will trust, believe, serve and give to whatever God does.

I love what Job says in Job 13:15a: "Though He slay me,

yet will I trust Him."

That's being relentless. That is saying "I am here for the long haul." That is laying down a marker. It is saying "I am not going anywhere, I am sticking around, no matter what happens." If you are going to learn to lead people who you want to be relentless, then you have to be an example. God will sometimes act as though He doesn't care, as though He has forgotten you, as though your prayers are of no interest to Him: stay relentless in your pursuit of Him. Trust Him, for He alone is trustworthy. He will work everything out for good. One day you will realise and appreciate His master plan for your life. We have to decide to let God be God and for us to be His servant, not His master.

QUOTES AND NOTES

Seven quotes on being *relentless*

1. Never give in, never give in, never, never, never, never.

Sir Winston Churchill

2. I have worked very hard to dedicate my personal and professional life to principle centred living. I am driven by a passion and conscience to spread understanding for principles and how to apply them to reach greatness. To that extent, there is no sacrifice—only a passionate, **relentless** commitment to my work, family, community and church to make a lasting difference.

Dr. Steven Covey

3. Leaders need to recognise the risks involved, but should never be afraid to make big decisions. They must pursue their mission with **relentless** determination.

Thueydides (on leadership)

4. **Relentless** leadership is embracing the fact that the need

for reinforcement never ends and uncomfortable conversations are a necessity. This is how we create something special.

Ralph Waldo Emerson

5. We don't give in and we don't stop. We are **relentless** and in the end we usually get where we want to be!

Gary Neville

6. The effort that has gone into building this team into what it is today has been **relentless!**

Jensen Button

7. I will not leave you or forsake you.

Joshua 1:5 (NKJV)

Seven notes on *being relentless*

List seven points from the chapter on **being relentless** which have struck you most and which you want to remember:

1..
....
2..
....
3..
....
4..
....
5..
....
6..
....
7..
....

Chapter Six

Learning to Trust

Who can you trust? That is a question I am often asked in relation to giving people authority and responsibility. In business I was always told to trust no one; that if you were going to get ahead, you kept your own counsel and kept your guard up. The fact is if you don't trust people then they in turn will not trust you.

The truth is: if your vision/organisation is going to grow, then at some stage you are going to have to trust some people.

When do you trust them? Do you begin to trust after three

months or six months? To play it safe, do you start to trust after one year or perhaps, to be really cautious, after five years? How long do you need with someone before you begin to trust them?

Trust is a very important issue! Too much trust too early with the wrong person can result in a bankrupt company, a split church, a dream turning into a nightmare.

Trust is something that is built over time. The Bible says to lay hands on no man suddenly (1 Timothy 5: 22). This means that we do not give the latest person who arrives on the scene responsibility before we have taken the time to get to know them. Many leaders spot a gifted person and immediately start to use that person and lay responsibility on them. The problem is we forget that a person's gift can take them places that their character cannot keep them. That person may be gifted but are they trustworthy?

In your learning to lead, learn to trust people appropriately.

There are 3 points to bear in mind when you are starting to learn how to trust:

- Trust slowly: inch by inch! Give a person whom you

don't know time, so that they can get to know you and you them. Simply put: if they are trustworthy for the first inch, give them a second inch and then a third. Soon this will turn into a foot and then, foot by foot, you will reach a yard. Trust takes time, but often we try to speed things up and short-cut the process. Take the route of patience, because adding the ingredient of time will help you discover who they are- their weaknesses and their strengths.

- Trust smoothly: have a smooth running organisation. Let it be known in your organisation that just because someone turns up, it does not mean they have the right to speak up. What I mean by that is: people need to earn the right to speak; they need to be willing to listen first before assuming they have a voice and influence. They need to learn the culture, the chemistry and the conviction of the leadership. I worry about people who have instant opinions when they are only five minutes through the door. Similarly, alarm bells ring in my mind when I meet people who seem overly spiritual and religious - those who have an answer for everything and give the impression they have a hot line to heaven. They worry me because they are not Biblical. Most characters I read about in my Bible had doubts, fears and concerns. They had good and bad days. They blew it. They made mistakes. So, do not let opinionated people disrupt the smooth running of your organisation. Do not let them intimidate you. If God has put you in charge, be in charge. Run your vision smoothly. Don't let anyone disrupt what you are trying to build.

- Trust smartly: when a new person comes around, paid or unpaid, use the first period of time wisely. Watch them in the little things. How they speak to you is one thing, but how do they speak to people whom they don't need to impress? What pleases them or annoys them? Listen to what they say about their last church, their last employment, their last wife/husband, their last 'situation'. As they speak, ask yourself the question: what are you telling me? Not only by what they say but also by what they do not say. Are they teachable, or do they already think they know everything?

Responsibility is easily given but not so easily taken away, so share it carefully. Can this person handle what you are going to give them? It is not their fault if they cannot; the fault is with you, because you decided to give them the 'ball' to carry, and if they drop it, it is because they were not ready.

A temptation, in the early days of an organisation, is to delegate responsibility without enough care and attention, without having built trust. You later pay for it with broken promises and broken lives.

Conversely, in the later days of an organisation, it is tempting to refuse to delegate responsibility because we give it too much care and attention. You then pay for it with an organisation that has lost its cutting edge and momentum.

There are six C's which, when used by you, ultimately communicate confidence.

The six C's are:

1. Competence

2. Calling

3. Commitment

4. Consistency

5. Character

6. Care

When these six C's are demonstrated they...

Communicate: Confidence!

Confidence is a two way street. Not only do you have to be wise and careful whom you trust, but you have to be aware that people are doing the exact same with you. They are checking you out as well. They are looking at your competence, checking out your calling, watching your commitment, observing your consistency, testing your character and taking care before they have confidence in you.

Some people do this within hours; some people take weeks, others take months, whilst others still take years. Will you stand the test of time?

You may have heard about what people say over time, regarding you and your vision. First of all they say:-

- "You'll never do it."

Then if you do it, they say:

- "It will never last."

When it lasts, they then say:

- "I always knew you could do it."

You need to give people time to trust you and you definitely need to take time to trust people.

There are many times when I have had high hopes for people in our organisation. Having followed the test of the C's with them and **nearly** ticked all the boxes, I have put them in positions of responsibility only to see them fall at the last hurdle. Time has proved that the test is worthwhile.

They may have had:

- Competence

- Calling

- Consistency

- Care

...but through a number of situations showed a lack of:

- Character and Commitment

You will learn to thank God for taking the time to trust,

because you will find it will save you a lot of pain.

I remember some people coming into our office, a number of years ago, and speaking to us about how, if we would just let them come alongside us in leadership and partnership, then they could be such a great help. The offer was refused. Beware of people who have a conditional commitment to you. They are not ready yet for leadership.

In fact beware of anyone who wants to march alongside you without marching first behind you. If God has made you the leader, then make sure you lead. Trust the trustworthy and mistrust the untrustworthy. Time and God will show you the difference.

One final thought on trust: learn quickly to trust God. This may seem elementary, but if you will trust Him above all others you will save yourself a lot of pain. We need to learn when and where to trust people, but we need to learn to trust God every time. He never lets you down. He never gives bad advice. He is always right. Before you ask others for their opinions make sure you have an idea of what you sense God is saying. You don't do anything in life publicly without everyone having an opinion. Make sure you have a sense of what God is saying before you hear what man is saying, otherwise you will find your head is turned by everyone's well intentioned advice.

Psalm 118:9 says: "It is better to trust in the Lord than to put confidence in man. It is better to trust in the Lord than to put confidence in princes."

Man will come and man will go, but God remains. Put your confidence firstly in Him and secondly in those whom you have learned to trust, those who have proven trustworthy.

QUOTES AND NOTES

Seven quotes on *trust*

1. Few delights can equal the presence of one whom we **trust** utterly.

George MacDonald

2. Never be afraid to **trust** an unknown future to a known God.

Corrie Ten Boom

3. A blessed thing it is for any man or woman to have a friend, one human soul whom we can **trust** utterly, who knows the best and worst of us, and who loves us in spite of all our faults.

Charles Kingsley

4.Love all, **trust** a few. Do wrong to none.

William Shakespeare

5. It is better to suffer wrong than to do it, and happier to be sometimes cheated than not to **trust.**

Samuel Johnson

6. Trust is the essence of leadership.

Colin Powell

7. Trust in the Lord with all your heart, and lean not on your own understanding.

Proverbs 3: 5

Seven notes on *trust*

List seven points from the chapter on **trust** which have struck you most and which you want to remember:

1..
....
2..
....
3..
....
4..
....
5..
....
6..
....
7..
....

Chapter Seven

Learning to Grow

Everyone thinks of changing the world, but no one thinks of changing himself!

Leo Tolstoy (Novelist)

If you do not learn, you will not grow. Growth as a leader is what drives the vision forward. If you are not growing, the people who work for you will catch up to you and if they remain with you, they will become stagnant.

- In a church this can make it religious

- In a business this makes it dangerous

- In a family this makes it vulnerable

I heard President George Bush say he read 92 books in a year at the White House as President of the United States. It challenged me to think I should read more - perhaps not 92 in a year - but maybe a few more than I currently read. May I encourage you to read a few more books too? If you decide to read that little bit more, you will have almost certainly decided to grow.

If a Jewish boy can memorise vast parts of the Old Testament and has the ability to conduct a sensible and in depth debate on Scripture, then that tells me that both you and I can study more.

Learning used to be finished at school, then it became college, then it was University; now it goes beyond your twenties, your thirties and on into mid-life and into old age. Learning should be a life-long activity.

Life will teach you something every day of the week, month and year, if you let it. People will teach you something new every day, if you will learn. The internet has vast volumes of information that could give your church/business/family a quantum leap.

Be honest now, do you think you know enough about that subject which people believe you are an expert in? You may know enough for yesterday or perhaps even today, but I can guarantee you that you do not know enough for tomorrow and thereafter.

If you are going to learn to lead then you are going to have to learn to learn, and through learning learn to grow!

You will need to discipline yourself to enable yourself to grow. Some experiences will have to wait. You will have to learn delayed gratification. You will need to learn sacrifice… including the sacrifice of being misunderstood. Compromise should become your enemy. Isolation can be your friend.

Any top sportsman will tell you that in order for them to be all that they potentially can be, they have to sacrifice. It means taking some people out of their lives and bringing others in.

What have you placed in your life to enable you to grow in your area of expertise?

Here are some pointers to consider:

• Books: Books, in some circles are going out of fashion.
People will say, 'I don't have the time',' I am too tired' or 'I
cannot afford to buy them'. First of all, you do have the
time. We all have the same time: 24 x 7 = 168 hours per
week. All Prime Ministers and Presidents and Kings and
Queens have the same time. Business leaders of multi-
national companies have the same amount of time. People
who have built large churches or large businesses have the
same amount of time. It's what you do with the time. How
you spend it. There are such things as talking books (or
audio books) to enable you to drive as you listen. There is
the internet, with its free content, and there are second-hand
books and libraries. Analyse your time for a week: where
you go, what you do, who you spend time with. You may
find that you are frittering your time away, or at least some
of it.

• People: There are people close to where you live, who are
further on than you are. They have done what you are
trying to do. Why not buy them a coffee, lunch or simply
invite them to your home for a one-on-one, where you can
take notes of their experiences, successes and failures? Any

leader worthy of the name will be prepared to invest in your future. That's what makes them a good leader. Suck them dry of their wisdom and their experience. They can save you a lot of pain. They are not your competitors, they are your enablers. Watch people every day, in every situation. Life will teach you so much as you live it. I love what Bishop T.D. Jakes' mother said to him when he was a boy:

> Life is a University, everyone is a teacher, when you get up in the morning, be sure you go to School.

• Conferences: When was the last time you took time out from the race to stock up and feed yourself? Conferences are great events to learn, share and compare notes with other leaders. As I write this, I also need to be honest: if you ask my wife she will tell you I almost always never want to go. I never want to leave the work behind; I never want to put down the immediate to invest in the future. However, if I don't take time out, I get blunt, I get drained, and I become less and less effective.

We all need times of refreshing, renewal and growth, and it comes through feeding. This feeding must not just be what you are comfortable with either. Check out other streams of thought apart from your own. You might not agree with everything they say, but let them challenge and provoke you in your thinking, and in your belief system. Expand your circles and contacts and bring fresh ideas into your work and ministry.

Conferences are great opportunities to take your eyes off your vision and let other people give you a bigger picture of what is going on in the world. You will almost always return to your work renewed and refreshed, with fresh energy and ideas for the next chapter and level of your work.

• Down time: You have to learn to rest, because rest can enable growth. If you don't believe me, observe children and how they are when they go through periods of rapid growth - they need more sleep and rest. Perhaps that explains why it is sometimes difficult to get your teenagers out of bed. They now have an excuse: they're growing!

Step One: You have to learn when to rest.

Step Two: You have to learn what makes you rest.

Step Three: You have to learn who to rest with.

Rest is important. When you have a dream, the temptation is to dream on, because you are living the dream. It consumes you and delights you. The dream and vision can become intoxicating though. It can isolate you and you have to learn to put it down and rest. The dream needs you to step away and see it from afar, where you can assess how it is progressing. What is it costing you - both you and your partner, and your family? Is the cost too high? Is it damaging your morals or your loved ones? There should always be a price that you will not pay. Sometimes the price is too high, and we need to step back and let it dawn on us that we are getting too close to the edge of the cliff. It is good, honourable and sensible to say 'thus far and no further' if we are about to go over the edge. If you don't step aside for rest, the **momentum** may take you over the cliff.

Now you are convinced that you need to rest, learn what makes you rest. Is it physical exercise, travelling, spending time with new people or old friends? What brings you to a place of peace? Perhaps it's reading a novel or an autobiography, or going to see a film. Whatever it is, find it, because you need it.

You also need to learn who to rest with. Samson, in the Bible, got into a lot of trouble when he laid his head down for rest and relaxation. Be careful where you lay your head, it might get you into trouble. You might even lose your hair! Seriously, who you rest with can be your healing but it also can be your hurting.

As you rest, you let your guard down, so you have to trust and be aware of whom you are with. Can you trust them? Can you trust yourself? Is it appropriate that you spend time with them? Coming down from the mountaintop of work and vision and from driving the dream forward, you need to be ready for what the valley brings. It can at first bring despair, disillusionment and unrest. This is perfectly normal as your body begins to relax and come away from the stress and strain. Temptation is never far away, as your body looks elsewhere for thrills and spills to get its usual intake of adrenalin. Resist the temptation and it will go. Don't resist it and your rest becomes regret! So be careful whom you are around and keep accountable to those you love.

There is some truth in the saying "work hard and play hard." Be as busy planning your playing as you are planning your work. Get a life sometimes. Go places where you can let your hair down and be yourself.

QUOTES AND NOTES

Seven quotes on *learning to grow*

1. One of the things that may get in the way of people being lifelong learners is that they're not in touch with their passion. If you're passionate about what it is you do, then you're going to be looking for everything you can to get better at it.

Jack Canfield

2. Live as if you were to die tomorrow, learn as if you were to live forever.

Mahatma Gandi

3. Your most unhappy customers are your greatest source of learning.

Bill Gates

4. Watch, listen and learn. You cannot know it all yourself...

anyone who thinks they do is destined for mediocrity.

Donald Trump

5. Leaders learn to lead as apprentices in the classroom of experience with senior leaders.

Ray Blunt

6. If a man's eye is on the eternal, his intellect will grow.

Ralph Waldo Emerson

7. Wisdom is the principal thing; therefore get wisdom. And in all your getting, get understanding.

Proverbs 4: 7

Seven notes on *learning to grow*

List seven points from the chapter on **learning to grow** which have struck you most and which you want to remember:

1...
....
2...
....
3...
....
4...
....
5...
....
6...
....
7...
....

Epilogue

We have worked our way through the seven principles of Learning to Lead. In our journey it has been my intention and desire to encourage, motivate and instruct you to believe that you have the capability to rise up and lead. I have no idea in what area God may use you in leadership. What I do know is that if you take the step I did and commit your future and your abilities to God, then you are in for the ride of your life.

I strongly suggest that you begin to practice the seven principles in your life. Look for opportunities to put into practice what you have learned. Everything you have gone through in your life to present can be used positively if you learn to submit it to God. He can take all your experiences good and bad and turn them into stepping stones to your future.

Please remember what I said about mistakes. Failure does not need to be final. Mistakes are made by everyone, but not everyone recovers. Make sure with God's help, you recover and move on.

Also remember the more light is shone upon you, the

more other distractions are attracted to you. I remember preaching and teaching in India. I was preaching one evening in an open air with all the spotlights on the stage. It seemed every bug and insect was making its way towards us on the stage. When I was speaking, I was swallowing all sorts of insects. I was struggling to keep focused because I was so aware of these flying attackers. The people in the darkness had no trouble at all, but for us in the light, we were tormented by every kind of insect. It is the same in leadership sometimes. The more you are in the light, the more heat is on you and the more various types of night life are attracted. Don't rush ahead wanting opportunities on bigger stages with bigger audiences, it all comes at a price. When you are ready God will promote you, never seek to self promote. It comes at too heavy a price.

Lastly I want to encourage you to let me know how this book has helped and encouraged you. I would love to hear about your leadership journey. If you are looking for further training materials or courses please make contact at the address below. We would love to help you in any way possible.

Let's learn to lead together.

contact@thefreedomcentre.com

www.learntolead.co

...so tell me more about the freedomcentre...?

freedomcentre is a church with a difference. We are a vibrant and creative church community from a wide mix of ages, cultures and backgrounds.

Jack & Sue McVicar
Senior Pastors and Founders

We get together on Sundays and throughout the week to worship and seek Jesus and to serve and love our community. We also have connections around the world including USA, India, Malaysia, and we have churches in Malawi, Africa. Based in Preston in the north west of England we run a variety of projects including: creative workshops, kids clubs, soup kitchens, mentoring, schools work, a retail shop and many others. We have converted a double decker bus which we use to work with young people, families and the vulnerable in our city.

To find out more about us, our projects and our year out opportunities contact us at
contact@thefreedomcentre.com

freedomcentre is a registered charity: 1106874

proclaim
GOOD NEWS
to the poor

BIND UP the
broken
hearted

proclaim
FREEDOM
to the
captives

www.thefreedomcentre.com

Our Vision...

Our name and vision come from Isaiah 61.

God gave us a dream and vision to build a centre that would bring together the church and the people God wants to reach

So what is our vision?

>> It is a centre that is used by the public and the church for varied purposes and needs.

>>It will be a powerful model of a worshipping, prayerful, supernatural church.

>> It will provide a variety of physical, business, retail, creative and spiritual needs.

>> It will reach the city of Preston, the nation and the nations in a variety of creative ways.

>> It will teach, train and mature balanced disciples sold out to Jesus.

>>It is to be a resource centre for local, national and international churches.

>>It will infiltrate and effect every stratum of city life in Preston